C000088815

ERNEST SHAC[

A Life from Beginning to End

Copyright © 2020 by Hourly History.

All rights reserved.

Table of Contents

Introduction

Ernest Shackleton was not just a great explorer of the Antarctic—he was also a great commander. When the chips were down, he could always be depended upon to put others ahead of himself. Time and time again, he proved to be a compassionate leader who made sure that he never left a single man behind on his expeditions. This compassionate concern for those under his charge was brilliantly evidenced in his famous journey to the Antarctic on the ship prophetically named the *Endurance*. The mission's main objective would prove to be a failure, but what Shackleton achieved in terms of common humanity was stunning all the same.

In this book, you will find presented in full the life, the legend, and the enduring spirit of one of the greatest adventurers this world has ever known—Sir Ernest Shackleton.

Chapter One

Early Life in Ireland

"I felt strangely drawn towards the mysterious south."

—Ernest Shackleton

Ernest Shackleton, the great explorer of Antarctica, was born on February 15, 1874, in Kilkea, Ireland. By the time he was around six years old, he moved with his family to the Irish capital of Dublin so that his father Henry—who was in his mid-thirties at the time—could train to become a medical doctor.

Ernest's care during these formative years was primarily left in the hands of a private teacher that the Shackletons had on hand, as Letitia, Ernest's mother, was too ill to take care of a household that eventually consisted of ten children. With his governess, Ernest learned the rudimentary basics of reading, writing, and arithmetic. Somewhere in the midst of all this learning, he also developed a keen sense of exploration, which the young Shackleton would put to use on his first exploration attempt—a voyage to Australia.

Ernest wanted to disembark from Ireland to Australia, and he wasn't going to do it by sea or air, but rather directly through the ground itself. The young Ernest was inspired to reach the great Down Under by digging a hole in his parents' garden. Obviously, he didn't reach Australia this way, but the sentiment the youngster displayed showcases the audacious roots of the budding explorer that Shackleton would one day become. Even though he wasn't able to tunnel to the other side of the world, the spark was lit, and he would forever keep this candle of ambition burning bright.

Chapter Two

Setting out to Sea

"My father thought to cure me of my desire for the sea by letting me go in the most primitive manner possible as a 'boy' on board a sailing ship at a shilling a month."

—Ernest Shackleton

At the age of 11, Ernest Shackleton's young life would become inundated with a heavy dose of change. His father, who had just completed his studies in medical school, had the whole family pack up and move across the Irish Sea to suburban London. Here Ernest was enrolled at a school called Fir Lodge.

Initially, Ernest had a difficult time adjusting. Although he was of English stock just like his peers, he had grown up in Ireland, and his classmates mercilessly tormented him over his Irish accent. Nevertheless, Ernest Shackleton persevered, and with the indomitable endurance that would mark much of his life, he managed to develop a thick skin when it came to childhood taunts. Soon enough, the very schoolmates that had picked on him, he had won over as his best of friends. In good time Ernest would come to excel in school both in and out of the classroom, and he developed a particular love of extracurricular sports, such as boxing and cricket.

The young Shackleton would leave Fir Lodge in 1887 in order to enroll at Dulwich College. He was 13 years old at the time and had already proved himself to be academically inclined, but even though he may have made good enough marks in his classes, his teachers couldn't help but feel that Ernest was holding out on them. Often enough, he would end up with report cards in which his instructors expressed this opinion by leaving the written notation of "could do better."

Despite his ability to score decent enough on tests and assignments, Ernest often appeared listless and uninterested in the classroom. His father, seeking to have Ernest prepped to follow in his footsteps as a physician, had arranged to have his coursework follow this path. This proved to be at odds with young Ernest's personal ambition, and as a result, he would sometimes exhibit a lackluster performance. In his spare time, Ernest was reading exciting magazines and periodicals that spoke of adventure in distant lands—and his determination to become just like the great explorers he read about only increased.

A few years prior, the stories Shackleton heard about had inspired him to dig a hole to Australia. He was now older and wiser and realized such a feat could not be done, but nevertheless, he wanted to hop on the first steamship bound for unknown ports all the same. As this sentiment became undeniably clear to his parents, by the time Ernest was 15, he had finally convinced them to give up any plans they had of molding him into a medical doctor. Instead, Henry and Letitia acquiesced to their son's dream of sailing the high seas by giving him their express permission to become a sailor. Their only stipulation was that he complete his schooling before he did so.

Although Ernest was not going to be a doctor as they had hoped, Henry and Letitia tried to make the best of their son's passion by having him apply to the Merchant Navy. Henry, through some of his relatives, helped Ernest to get a spot on a ship called the *Hoghton Tower*. The young Ernest then fulfilled his part of the bargain with phenomenal speed as he went on to not only finish his schooling but to suddenly do so well that he was placed fifth in his class. Acing his exams, Ernest got his affairs in order and quickly headed off to the port city of Liverpool, where he eagerly took his place on the *Hoghton Tower* at the tender age of 16.

The ship's first destination was for Valparaiso, Chile. It wasn't exactly headed for Shackleton's future claim to fame of Antarctica, but as one of the closest regions on Earth to the South Pole, it was going in that direction all the same.

For the first time in his young life, Shackleton was taking charge of his own destiny. In those early days, he was truly a free spirit, but perhaps he occasionally took pause to think of those instructors who had written "could do better" on his report cards. Just maybe, as he stood on the open deck of the *Hoghton Tower* with the sun on his face and a cool breeze ruffling his hair, he thought to himself that they had been absolutely right. Now that he had set sail and chartered a course to make his dreams a reality, it couldn't get much better than this.

Chapter Three

Rounding Cape Horn

"I called to the other men that the sky was clearing, and then a moment later I realized that what I had seen was not a rift in the clouds but the white crest of an enormous wave."

—Ernest Shackleton

From the very beginning of his journey to Chile on the *Hoghton Tower*, the life of a sailor proved to be a daunting one. The vessel was a fast-moving clipper ship, and Shackleton had to stay alert while he learned the ropes of how the craft was operated. There were over 200 ropes in fact that were responsible for the operation of the vessel, which all went into play when it came to orienting the huge sails that propelled the ship. As part of Shackleton's role in this maintenance, he often had to ascend the masts of the ship. Even during bad storms, Ernest found himself up high, clinging to the rigging, while adjusting the ropes. It was a hard job, but Shackleton took to it well, enjoying the difficulty as part of the adventure he was on.

The most rigorous part of his journey was when the *Hoghton Tower* traveled around the very tip of South America in order to maneuver around to Chile. Cape Horn was known for its horrible weather conditions, and during this difficult passage, Shackleton observed just how much turbulence a ship like the *Hoghton Tower* could face and still be able to right itself. During this treacherous trip, the ship experienced one bad squall after another, getting pushed and battered around, all while seeking to avoid a direct collision with any icebergs that had made their way from the Antarctic.

It was his brush with the extremes near the tip of South America that would be the most eventful part of his voyage. After making a stop in Chile, the mighty *Hoghton Tower* would then head back to Britain, disembarking in Liverpool in April of 1891. Ernest was only 17 years old at the time and still young enough to be able to change his mind if he had found his experience at sea to be too much for him. But on the contrary, his experience—hardship and all—had only solidified his determination that he was indeed on the right path in life.

Shackleton enjoyed the rigors that he had experienced as much as he loved the feeling of being on the go. As such, he renewed his contract on the *Hoghton Tower*, setting his sights on rising through the ranks. In these efforts, Shackleton would repeat the trip around South America's Cape Horn on numerous occasions. During his journeys, he would become acquainted with men from all manner of backgrounds. Even though it was not typical for young men seeking to become officers to associate with lower-level sailors, Shackleton defied social protocol and became the best of friends even with the lowest ranking ship hands. It was for this reason among others that the crew began to call Ernest "Old Shacks."

In 1894, at the age of just 20 years old, Shackleton did indeed pass his examinations to become an officer, earning for himself the rank of second mate. This enabled him to get a place for himself on board the *Monmouthshire*, a prestigious steamship that hauled shipments to several places, including locales in East Asia and South America. As he rose through the ranks, for Ernest Shackleton, it was always full steam ahead.

Chapter Four

Denied His Love

"I seemed to vow to myself that someday I would go to the region of ice and snow and go on till I came to one of the poles of the earth, the end of the axis upon which the great round ball turns."

—Ernest Shackleton

During his time on board the steamer called the *Monmouthshire*, Ernest Shackleton visited ports far and wide, hauling freight as far east as China and Japan. He came back to Britain shortly after the new year of 1896 and began taking exams to attain the ranking of first mate. He succeeded in these efforts and was then placed as part of the crew of the *Flintshire* where he undertook a seven-month tour of duty.

Although Shackleton had already achieved much upon his return to Britain in 1897, he began to think in terms of not just career success, but also personal success. He longed to have a companion with whom to share all his triumphs. A woman by the name of Emily Dorman was the one who presented herself to answer the call of Shackleton's longing. Ms. Dorman was already a familiar face around the Shackleton family since she was a friend of Ernest's sister Kathleen. Although she was a full six years older than Ernest, she was strikingly beautiful with her dark hair and tall, trim figure. Besides that, the two also had common interests in things such as poetry and literature.

The pair soon began to speak of marriage, but Emily's father was hesitant due to Ernest's young age and lack of reliable income. Even though he was a first-class officer, the money he earned was rather spotty at best and considered not stable enough for him to take on a bride.

The fact that his love was denied him was a troubling blow, but as he shipped out again, Shackleton sought to put the disappointment to the side as he buried himself back in his work at sea. Nevertheless, he still wrote Emily whenever he could, and the two developed a long correspondence in which they continued to express their love and admiration for each other and the hope that someday they would be able to become husband and wife.

Ernest knew full well that the biggest objection Emily's father had of him was due to his lack of finances. He did not take this rebuke lying down; instead, he sought to do something about it. In 1898, Shackleton took even further examinations that would place in him the rank of master. This was a position that would most certainly open doors for him as it allowed him to command just about any ship that sailed for the British Empire.

This was certainly a welcome development, but still, Shackleton wanted more. He knew that he would never be happy leading mundane shipments day in and day out. Seeking a vocation that would be a little bit more exciting, he applied and was hired on for the sought-after Union-Castle Line, which delivered mail freight from Britain to posts in South Africa.

This position also had the extra advantage of allowing Ernest to have more downtime in England so that he could pay frequent visits to Emily. He became a regular fixture in Emily's life, but to Ernest's chagrin, her father still didn't seem to approve of their relationship. No matter what Shackleton did, he couldn't seem to convince Mr. Dorman to grant him the right to wed his daughter.

For Ernest, rounding Cape Horn must have seemed an easier proposition than having to navigate through the displeasure of the Dorman family patriarch. Temporarily unable to succeed in this personal conquest, Shackleton would soon set his sights on a more temporal one—in the uncharted waters of the Antarctic.

Chapter Five

First Expedition to Antarctica

*"The noise resembles the roar of heavy, distant surf.
Standing on the stirring ice one can imagine it is disturbed
by the breathing and tossing of a mighty giant below."*

—Ernest Shackleton

Right at the turn of the century, in early 1900, Ernest
Shackleton made a fateful trip to South Africa that would
forever change his life. It was during the course of this trip
that Shackleton met a man by the name of Cedric
Longstaff. Cedric was a fresh recruit headed for the Boer
War that Britain was fighting on the African continent at
the time. It was a simple remark that Cedric made about his
father Llewellyn, a rich British industrialist, that really got
Ernest's attention. Shackleton knew of Llewellyn because
he was the main financial backer behind the National
Antarctic Expedition. Llewellyn Longstaff championed the
cause of Britain returning to Antarctica after being absent
from the continent for about 60 years.

Britain had first gone to the Antarctic in 1841. Their
return to the region after so many decades was something
akin to what it would be like for the United States to return
to the Moon several decades after the Apollo missions to

the lunar surface had come and gone. This was precisely the ambitious scheme that Llewellyn Longstaff supported—and the very notion excited young Ernest Shackleton to no end. As such, he asked his newfound friend Cedric to beseech his father on his behalf to consider him for the venture. Cedric wrote a formal introduction of Ernest to his father and requested the man to meet up with him.

Upon his return to British soil, the meeting was arranged, and Ernest Shackleton laid his case to the wealthy financer as to why he should allow him to join the expedition to Antarctica. Llewellyn was amazed by the young man's passion and soon agreed to be of assistance. By the time Ernest returned to Britain again in March of 1901, he was officially made a part of the National Antarctic Expedition under the aegis of veteran sailor, geographer, and explorer Clements Markham.

Markham put Shackleton under the direction of Robert Falcon Scott, who was a torpedo lieutenant for the Royal Navy at the time and who would be commanding the ship to the Antarctic. Scott, in turn, had Shackleton placed in the administration of the preparation of the seafaring vessel, which was aptly named the *Discovery*. With a timetable of just six months before the fateful venture was to be made, Shackleton had his hands quite full in his efforts of making sure that the *Discovery* was well stocked, supplied, and seaworthy.

The ship was a massive hybrid of old-fashioned sails as well as powerful steam engines, deemed to be necessary to persevere through turbulent waters, gale-force winds, and incessant, freezing rain of the Antarctic. Most importantly, it had to be able to cut its way across the thick pack of sea ice that surrounded the Antarctic continent. Once the ship was determined to be seaworthy, Shackleton could then focus on more monotonous tasks such as stocking coal, warm clothes, and food for the expedition.

It was after all of these preparations were made that on July 31, 1901, the *Discovery* disembarked from London and headed out on its journey into the open water southward bound to the bottom of the world, Antarctica. Among those present to wish Shackleton well at his departure was his long-time love Emily. Ernest had been regaling her for several weeks about his hopes for fame and fortune at the South Pole. He felt that his success was all but guaranteed—Emily, however, was not so sure. Nevertheless, she put on a brave face and kissed her stalwart champion of the open ocean goodbye.

Chapter Six

A Race against Death

"We had seen God in His splendors, heard the text that Nature renders. We had reached the naked soul of man."

—Ernest Shackleton

After leaving Britain, the crew of the *Discovery* had a rather monotonous journey ahead of them, filled mostly with daily chores, tasks, and whatever they could muster to keep themselves entertained. The main concern for the voyage that seemed to override everything else was to conserve the ship's supply of coal as much as possible. The craft was to use the natural winds filling its sails as its primary driver and only the coal when there was no wind to be found. The coal, of course, would be much needed once they reached the rigors and tempestuous environs of the Antarctic; so, the more they managed to hang onto in their stores for the challenging final leg of the journey, the better.

The crew reached the shores of Madeira—a group of autonomous Portuguese islands—in August before beginning the trip toward Cape Town, South Africa. From here, the crew journeyed on to South Trinidad, where they stayed ashore for several hours on September 13. The ship was then eventually sailed to the southside of Australia in mid-November where they encountered their first batch of heavy sea ice. Cutting through these natural surface features, the ship bounded forward to New Zealand, where the crew arrived at Lyttleton at the end of the month.

Shackleton was in high spirits at the time that he and his crew left Lyttleton on December 21, but the jubilant departure was much overshadowed when one of his crewmembers tripped and fell to his death from a masthead. Luckily, the rest of the journey commenced rather uneventfully, and it was right after the New Year of 1902 had dawned that Shackleton and crew crossed the pack ice of the Antarctic and sailed on into the Ross Sea.

Once across these treacherous waters, they then landed at Cape Adare, the tip of a northeastern Antarctic peninsula discovered by James Clark Ross in his landmark expedition in 1841. Upon landfall, Shackleton disembarked with several other men and began busying himself with collecting rocks and lichens as well as taking several photos of other intriguing finds, such as a crew favorite— the mischievous antics of the polar penguins that frolicked about.

The animals that proved of greatest interest, however, were the seals that surfaced off the coast since it was through the hunting of these creatures that the crew managed to provide extra meat for the hungry seamen. The ship continued around the coast until they reached Granite Harbour on January 19. Here, they disembarked once again to explore the icy environment.

During this foray, the crew soon made a groundbreaking discovery in the form of a large patch of moss. This was important to the scientific aspect of the mission since no such vegetation had been previously found. After this discovery, the crew returned to their craft and continued their trajectory along the eastern edge of Antarctica. Here they encountered ice cliffs that ascended hundreds of feet.

Another major find was recognized by the crew on January 30, when they reached a veritable wall of ice. The ship was able to dock in an inlet in this Great Ice Barrier, where the team could gather their wits and their scientific equipment in order to conduct a few experiments. It was here that the crew inflated a balloon on February 4 and had Shackleton step aboard to go aloft to see what he could see. This was, of course, after commander Robert Falcon Scott was given the honor.

Once given the opportunity to ascend over the polar region, Shackleton didn't waste it. Floating several feet above the Barrier, Shackleton took photos of the ice wall from his vantage point in the balloon, very much lending aid in the efforts to identify important surface features.

By early February, it was determined that a southerly passage near Mount Erebus would be the most likely way forward toward the South Pole. But first, the crew would have to wait out the harsh winter. They did so by parking their craft off the coast of Ross Island. During this time, the crew vigorously prepared for their upcoming landing expedition. This they did through the building of so-called observation huts as well as the great hut that would serve as a kind of headquarters.

The first sledding expedition took place in the middle of February in search of a southerly route to the Barrier. This trek was put on hold when the group ran headlong into a bad blizzard and were forced to stay put in the middle of a sheet of ice. They were stuck like this for several hours, and it is said that just about everyone there suffered to some degree from frostbite as the temperature plummeted. When the sun came up the next morning, conditions were not that much better. The men found that their boots were frozen solid, making putting them on a frightful task.

Nevertheless, they marched on, and as they continued their journey south toward the pole, they eventually found that they were not walking on sea ice but on solid glacier ice, which of course meant that they had ventured onto the Great Ice Barrier itself. Yet they only made it so far before the elements forced them to turn back and return to their encampment upon the ice—and then to the *Discovery* itself.

Here, they passed the winter months as best they could with routine chores, food, conversation, and even a periodical newspaper called *The South Polar Times*, edited by Ernest Shackleton himself, which was passed around among the crew. This was how the crew of the *Discovery* passed their days until the real journey toward the South Pole would begin on November 2, 1902.

It was on the morning of November 2 that Shackleton, the ship's physician Dr. Edward Wilson, and Captain Robert Falcon Scott set out on three separate sleds with some twenty dogs total between them. On the first day of this trek, the group logged about 12 miles. Soon after this, however, a heavy snowstorm hit, causing the group of intrepid explorers to seek refuge in a tent out on the open ice. Having to wait it out, it would be a couple of days before the three men would begin moving again, and by the November 15, their supporting party—the group of helpers that had thus far joined them—turned around and headed back for the *Discovery*. Shackleton and company then continued their trek, covering about 15 miles per day.

As they progressed, Shackleton's health soon began to decline, and due to severe coughing fits, he was not allowed to lead the sled. At this point, he also began to show clear indications of having contracted a bad case of scurvy. Food was quickly running out, and the men tried to ration their meals best they could. Meanwhile, the dogs fell ill because their diet was even worse, consisting only of spoiled fish. Throughout the trek, the men killed off the dogs for meat, and by the time they reached their farthest point on December 30, almost all the dogs were dead. None would make it back to the *Discovery*.

The three explorers had gone farther south than any man before, beating the old record by more than 200 miles. Still, Shackleton was disappointed when they were forced to begin the grueling journey back to the ship. He was sick and utterly worn out. It was bad enough, in fact, that it was decided that as soon as they returned to the *Discovery*, Shackleton should be placed on a relief ship, a Norwegian sealer by the name of *Morning*, and escorted away from Antarctica. Shackleton was devastated to have to abort his mission, but in the end, he had no choice in the matter. The journey had very nearly killed him. After everything he had tried so hard to accomplish, Ernest Shackleton had no choice but to turn around and go home.

Chapter Seven

Work for the Royal Geographical Society

"I want to go on a further expedition soon. This time I want to command it myself."

—Ernest Shackleton

Even as the frozen coastline of Antarctica faded from view from his vantage point on the relief ship, Shackleton was vowing to himself that he would be back to the Antarctic. But first, he had to successfully leave. The *Morning* demonstrated that this was no easy task as the ship was forced to continually weave and dodge through a minefield of floating icebergs when it departed on March 2, 1903.

Shackleton would remember his rescue as being something akin to "steering a bicycle through a graveyard." He was nevertheless extracted from Antarctica, and with nothing more for him to do, he would convalesce on the craft that had rescued him until he safely arrived at the shores of New Zealand on March 19. He continued to rest in New Zealand for a few more months before leaving in early May on a ship called the *Orotava*, which would take him to San Francisco, then to New York, before finally coming to rest in Britain in June.

Upon re-joining his social circle in Britain, Shackleton became a ceaseless advocate for further exploration of the Antarctic. Equipped with the photographs he had taken, he vividly described all that he had borne witness to during his journey to the South Pole. He even gave riveting lectures on the subject for the Royal Geographical Society.

Momentous change occurred in Shackleton's personal life as well, with Emily finally coming around to the prospect of marrying him. Her father had already passed on, so the decision was all hers to take. As a consequence of her father's death, she had also received a hefty inheritance that she was more than willing to share with Shackleton. Ernest bristled at the notion of others believing that his marriage to Emily was simply to gain access to her wealth. Emily, on the other hand, had no pretensions about her intent to aid her husband financially. In her mind, the fact that she could pay the more routine bills enabled Ernest to pursue his dreams rather than eking out a living just to get by, or as she herself said, "One must not chain down an eagle in a barnyard."

Shortly after Ernest's return, it was the Royal Scottish Geographical Society which presented itself as this great eagle's next most likely perch. Shackleton was already acquainted with the work of the group, and when he received word that there was an opening in the post for secretary, he swooped right in. After a nerve-wracking wait, on January 11, 1904, Shackleton was informed that he had indeed been selected to serve as secretary. This position, which came with a modest amount of pay, helped to give Shackleton the clout and respect that being a weather-beaten explorer could not provide. It was in his elected role as secretary of the RSGS that Shackleton was finally able to silence some of the remaining naysayers in Emily's family who may have disapproved of their union.

With this bit of respectability squared away, Ernest and Emily were finally wed on April 9, 1904. For their home, the newlyweds chose a modest house on the edge of Edinburgh from whence Ernest could easily commute to his office with the RSGS. With the help of his wife, who was already a known figure in high society, it wasn't long before Ernest Shackleton too began to climb the social ladder.

In the midst of all this hobnobbing, Shackleton received word of Robert Falcon Scott's triumphant return from Antarctica. The fact that he had been the one to abruptly return home while Scott had braved it out for the duration of the mission weighed heavily on Shackleton, but he was determined to remain cordial with Scott all the same. He even delivered a friendly invitation for Scott to speak at the RSGS, but the goodwill would prove to be short-lived when Shackleton received word that Scott had been referring to his efforts in the Antarctic in some rather unflattering terms. In particular, he spoke of the fact that Shackleton had to be pulled on a sled while he was severely incapacitated.

While Shackleton openly acknowledged the physical hardship he had suffered, he never imagined that he would be portrayed in such a manner. He would long hold Scott in contempt for the way that he described his first great foray toward the South Pole. But much more than being unhappy with Scott's version of events, it ignited a fire within Shackleton to prove Scott and everyone else wrong—and the only way he would be able to do it would be to set sail back to Antarctica.

Chapter Eight

Business Ventures and Political Aspirations

"Superhuman effort isn't worth a damn unless it achieves results."

—Ernest Shackleton

Shackleton was still hoping to make a name for himself by going back to the Antarctic, but in November of 1904, another means of potential name recognition came his way in the form of a political bid in Parliament. Despite the slights and jabs at his character received from Scott, Shackleton was still a popular public figure, and he seemed to have a natural gift for oratory. He was also considered a political asset because of his Irish heritage.

The most contentious issue of the day was whether or not Ireland should have Home Rule. The debate over how much autonomy Ireland should have from the rest of the United Kingdom had raged for several years. Shackleton jumped right into the fray of this controversy, voicing his opposition to Home Rule. As he stated at the time, "I am an Irishman, and I consider myself a true patriot when I say that Ireland should not have Home Rule."

The fact that Shackleton was stepping into the political limelight was not lost on his colleagues with the RSGS, however, and he was duly informed that indulging in politics while on their payroll was not looked kindly upon. As the pressure upon Shackleton built, it became clear that he might be dismissed from the organization. It was when the writing was all but on the wall that Shackleton took the initiative and resigned in early 1905.

While Ernest Shackleton was on the campaign trail, his wife Emily gave birth to a rambunctious baby boy named Raymond. Ernest thought his son to have the fighting spirit from the very beginning, and upon first seeing him, he is said to have looked at his little balled up hands and exclaimed, "Good fists for fighting!" Shackleton, always feeling like the underdog himself, could most certainly relate to the idea of having to fight from birth for recognition and respect.

Shortly after the birth of his son and while continuing his campaign for a seat in Parliament, Shackleton attempted to put as many irons into the fire as possible, hoping that one business opportunity or another would allow him to hit it big. One of these ventures occurred as a result of the Russo-Japanese War that had come to its conclusion in 1905. In this conflict, the Russians were delivered a decisive defeat at the hands of the Japanese, and as a consequence, the ill-prepared Russians suddenly found huge segments of their army trapped in the Far East without a way home. It was in answer to this plight that some— Shackleton included—saw a potential opportunity.

When it was made known that the Russians were attempting to escort 40,000 soldiers from Vladivostok, back through the Black Sea at a rate of 40 pounds per transported troop, Ernest Shackleton was all ears. He readily proclaimed, "My 1,000 shares will be worth 4,000 pounds in a few days." He thought that he had finally found a way to put him and Emily on easy street, and he told her as much at the time, declaring to her that "things will be alright with us forever."

However, just a short time later, the deal on which Ernest had placed so much faith had completely collapsed. Back once again at square one, Shackleton began to look into several business opportunities in and around London. His wife Emily, meanwhile, had become pregnant with their second child. As an older mother already reaching into middle age, the pregnancy was of great concern to them both. Fortunately for the Shackletons, Emily was able to persevere and give birth to a healthy, happy baby girl by the name of Cecily on December 23, 1906.

All in all, Ernest had failed in his Russian enterprises, and after the campaign season was over, he had dismally failed to gain a seat in Parliament. Yet this one successful delivery allowed the embattled Ernest Shackleton to end the year on a much-needed high note.

Chapter Nine

Return to Antarctica

"Difficulties are just things to overcome after all."

—Ernest Shackleton

By the time the year 1907 had rolled around, Shackleton was in desperate need of a change. Too many of his old leads had turned into dead ends, and he needed a new outlet for his ambition. He found this outlet in the form of the British industrialist William Beardmore.

Beardmore had hired Shackleton on with his firm to serve in a role as a kind of roving commissioner, who was sent out to conduct question-and-answer sessions with wealthy people and organizations that might be someday inclined to conduct business with Beardmore. Many of these proposed ventures that Shackleton worked on as Beardmore's agent involved faraway places that companies sought to extract rare resources from. Places such as the Yukon territory were solicited in order to convince wealthy magnates to expend their resources for expeditions to retrieve these rare materials. It was in this vein that Shackleton began to openly speak once again of the value he believed could be gleaned from a return to Antarctica.

These overtures then led to Shackleton presenting his case directly to the Royal Geographical Society in February of 1907. Once the mission was approved, Shackleton began to advertise it as the official British Antarctic Expedition, 1907. With this simple but effective title, Shackleton sought to stir up patriotism as well as a feeling of being on the cusp of something altogether new, just waiting to break out in the brand-new year of 1907.

He touted the main objective of this mission to be in search of both the geographical and the magnetic South Pole. At first, it seemed that Shackleton was simply recreating the mission that he had conducted with the crew of the *Discovery* a few years prior. Indeed, he had already attempted to enlist many of these former crew members, but when they failed to show any interest, he realized that he really was going to have to start from scratch. He soon turned to "amateurs and gentlemen adventurers like himself." It was from this group that he cobbled together the complete team that would revolve around his leadership. Seemingly making things official, Shackleton was then made a member of the Royal Victorian Order. It was from here that Shackleton arranged for the ship, the *Nimrod*, to set sail for the Antarctic.

Perhaps revealing just how much planning went into such an endeavor, the fact that the ship for a mission entitled British Antarctic Expedition, 1907 did not set sail until early 1908 shows just how long it took to get affairs in order.

With this launch, Shackleton was free to explore, but it still came with one glaring stipulation. Since his return from the Antarctic, Scott had demanded that the McMurdo Sound region, which he had already claimed for himself, be off-limits for any future missions. As frustrated as

Shackleton may have been with Scott, he agreed to honor that request.

Upon disembarking from its port, the *Nimrod* was initially towed some 1,650 miles by a steamer in order to conserve as much coal as possible. Such a feat was indicative that this time around, Shackleton was not taking much of anything for granted. As the craft reached polar waters, true to his word, Shackleton made sure that they steered clear of the McMurdo Sound and headed for the eastern side of the Great Ice Barrier instead.

The *Nimrod* arrived at its destination on January 21, 1908. Here they were quick to discover that this area had since turned into a kind of inlet in which a whole horde of whales had made their home. It was for this reason that Shackleton named the region the aptly fitting title of the Bay of Whales. It wasn't long before the crew of the *Nimrod* was moving on, however, when they realized that the immediate climate found in the Bay of Whales was much to tumultuous for them to form a stable bridgehead.

From here, Shackleton and company sought to find a new landing site off the shores of King Edward VII Land, but this turned into a miserable failure as well. It was for this reason that Shackleton felt compelled to break his oath to Scott and make landfall in the McMurdo Sound instead. Some would later say that Shackleton did such a thing out of sheer spite, but others would affirm that it was simply a matter of common sense considering the difficult ice conditions.

At any rate, the *Nimrod* entered the sound on January 29 but was once again diverted from its objective on account of the ice that they encountered some 16 miles from what had been the *Discovery*'s previous encampment of Hut Point. The crew persevered, and after braving the elements for a few more days, they managed to set anchor a few miles further out at Cape Royds. The crew had already faced much rigor and hardship but nevertheless were said to have been in high spirits. Perhaps the man who was in the highest of spirits was Shackleton himself. Despite the difficulty, in his mind, he was on his way to finally complete his mission once and for all.

Chapter Ten

Journey toward the South Pole

"If I had not some strength of will I would make a first-class drunkard."

—Ernest Shackleton

After spending several months at their base camp, the crew had become fairly well acquainted with each other. Most of these relations appeared to be quite cordial, but there is one account about an alleged falling out between Ernest Shackleton and the *Nimrod*'s naval steward, Captain Rupert England. It was alleged that in light of England learning that Shackleton was considering his release on account of ill health, a tussle broke out between the two men in which England attempted to rip a telegraph out of Shackleton's hand.

This supposedly resulted in a brief scuffle that left both of the men on the floor. It is worth noting, however, that shortly after this incident allegedly occurred, both men emphatically denied its occurrence. In fact, once the rumor of this altercation was out, Shackleton even went so far as to circulate a letter denying the incident amongst the crew and had everyone sign it—in apparent solidarity in this supposed non-event.

At any rate, by early March, the group began their ascent up Mount Erebus. They made good time up the mountain and were only stalled when, on March 9, a blizzard broke out that left them temporarily stuck in place. Nevertheless, the goal of climbing Mount Erebus's lower, main crater was a success, allowing the crew to return to their base camp with at least this one small triumph at their disposal.

After this feat, Shackleton had his men prepared to hunker down for the south polar winter, which would last until late September. During all of this downtime, many scientific experiments were conducted by examining microscopic lifeforms found in the polar ice and through the study of magnetism and atmospheric phenomenon such as the aurora. Along with these groundbreaking studies, the more practical matter of preparing gear and animals consumed much of the crew's time.

It is said that during all of this, Shackleton was front and center, always ready to help with any task, whether it was in the aid of a meteorological experiment or the training of dogs for the sleds. Shackleton proved himself to be a dependable leader, and it seemed during these few months of preparation that every fiber of his being was dedicated to the journey to come.

It was in the morning hours of Thursday, October 29, 1908, that Shackleton and crew left their base camp and began their long, arduous march toward the South Pole. Shackleton's journal was confident and joyous as he marked the occasion with the entry, "A glorious day for our start. Brilliant sunshine and a cloudless sky."

The main group of explorers, consisting of Ernest Shackleton, Frank Wild, Eric Marshall, and Jameson Adams, left with four ponies between them to help pull their sleds, as well as a small supporting party of six additional crewmen who pulled their own gear. The ponies, in particular, proved difficult to use on the uneven surface of the Antarctic. In many instances, the group found itself delayed when one of these diminutive horses became hampered by a crevasse in the snowy ice.

The weather meanwhile was just as unpredictable as usual, and though the polar winter was technically over, snowstorms could still flare up at a moment's notice, as was the case when a bad blizzard struck on November 5, forcing the group to hunker down in their tents to wait out the storm. Shortly thereafter, however, the group picked up and continued their progress across the snowy desert. Making good time, by November 19, they had reached farther inland than Shackleton's previous expedition had managed to do by mid-December.

As happy as the group was, a few days later, they had to deal with the setback of one of their ponies perishing in the snow. Ever resourceful, Shackleton immediately made sure that the beast was butchered and its meat saved for future use. This setback was followed by another one of similar proportions on November 28, when another horse become so listless it had to be put down. The group, left with just two horses, now had to rely on manpower much more often than horsepower. Under these conditions, the group of intrepid explorers trudged on until, on December 2, they reached the summit of an outcropping that perhaps reflecting their own aspirations for good fortune, Mount Hope.

Another milestone was reached on December 5, when the group reached the so-called Lower Glacier Depot, opening wide their path to the South Pole. A couple of days later, however, one of the men of Shackleton's team nearly fell to his death when the pony that had been leading his sled fell through the ice. When the horse fell through, it very nearly took the man and his sled with it, but with a struggle, both man and sled were freed. The group, with just one beast of burden left between them, continued their laborious trek.

Their greatest achievement would occur on January 1, 1909, when they broke in the new year by breaking all previous records of an inland march toward the South Pole. Commemorating how far they had come, on January 9, the group planted the British flag at what was then known as the Farthest South latitude reached toward the South Pole.

Despite breaking these records, Shackleton wished to go even farther. But as the weather worsened and the condition of his crew weakened, it was determined that enough was enough, and the brave group of explorers decided to turn back. It would take several weeks before they managed to return to their old encampment and await their retrieval. The *Nimrod* picked up the weary men on March 1, thereby bringing Shackleton's second attempt to conquer the South Pole to its conclusion.

Chapter Eleven

Shipwrecked on an Ice Floe

"Optimism is true moral courage."

—Ernest Shackleton

Ernest Shackleton and his crew arrived off the coast of New Zealand's Stewart Island on March 23, 1909. He was received as a hero, and as soon as his exploits hit the telegraph wires in London, all of the British Empire were enamored with his efforts.

The true hero's welcome would come when Ernest Shackleton arrived in London in mid-June. Here he was greeted with praise from all corners of British society. On July 10, he was even received by none other than King Edward VII himself, who saw to it that Shackleton was officially knighted for his efforts of bringing glory and prestige to the Crown. It seemed that Ernest had finally achieved the acclaim that he had for so long sought.

Even with all of this acclaim, however, Shackleton found himself to be a man very much in debt. Unable to pay the debtors he owed for the mission, he was forced to request and was given a grant of some 20,000 pounds to pay the most daunting of them. His exploits had most certainly brought him fame, but fortune as these dire financial straits indicate had remained elusive.

So, what was Shackleton's solution to these pressing matters? Another expedition, of course. As such, it wasn't long before Shackleton was calling for renewed support so that he could lead another team to the planet's southernmost pole. Shackleton spent the next few years championing this cause along with attempts at various business ventures that never really got off the ground.

In the meantime, as Shackleton's star began to wane, a Norwegian team stunned the world by being the first to reach the actual physical spot of the South Pole in late 1911. (A party led by Robert Falcon Scott was the second to reach the South Pole, although they all perished on the journey back to their ship.) With this objective reached by a foreign power, Shackleton realized that the only other first left to be achieved would be to send a team on a Trans-Arctic Expedition, taking them from one side of the Antarctic to the other. Such a feat would be twice as hard as reaching the pole, but Shackleton was determined to do it all the same. He would need another seaworthy craft to do so and thus began to keep his eye out for vessels that might fit this bill.

As it turned out, just such a craft by the tell-tale name of *Polaris* had been constructed in late 1913. This ship was touted to be one of the strongest ships ever built for ice. The only trouble was its specifications made it sort of a misfit in the market. It lacked proper cargo space to be of interest to sealers, and it wasn't luxurious enough to be a yacht. The ship was really only good for one thing, and one thing only—an expedition to the South Pole. With no takers, by early 1914, the owners of *Polaris* were desperate to sell it. By the time Shackleton expressed interest, the sellers were ready to part with the ship for just 11,000 pounds. Upon acquiring the craft, Shackleton renamed the vessel *Endurance*, hoping to channel just such fortitude in his plans for a renewed expedition to Antarctica.

The ship would set sail for this new mission with Shackleton's handpicked crew in August 1914, but Shackleton himself would not go with them. Having to tie up some loose ends on the home front, he would meet them nearly a full month later in September, having sailed separately to the port of Buenos Aires. In the meantime, the whole world had become embroiled in the catastrophic conflict that would become known as World War I. No one at the time realized how bad the war would get at its outset, but Shackleton figured it was of no consequence to his mission.

He was proven mistaken because, after docking in what was at the time a neutral pot in Madeira, the *Endurance* found itself waylaid by a German craft. The German ship had apparently collided with the *Endurance*, and its crew believed that it had been done on purpose. War or no war, this was an affront that the captain of the *Endurance*— Worsley—was not going to take lying down. Incredibly enough, the very next morning, he led a boarding party onto the German craft and rounded up the engineers and forced them to fix the damage that they had caused. With engagements like this, even before Ernest Shackleton stepped aboard the ship, the *Endurance* and her crew were already developing quite a reputation.

It wouldn't be until October that the *Endurance* would pick up Shackleton from South America. With Shackleton on board, the ship would then arrive at a port in South

Georgia Island on October 26. While there, Shackleton sought to make some final preparations, as well as rest up a bit before the real journey began.

The *Endurance* would leave South Georgia on December 5. It was slow going from here, as the ice seemed thicker than had been expected. The surrounding water was also fast freezing around them. Things would then go from bad to worse when on January 19, 1915, the ship became completely moribund in a quick freeze. Shackleton and company armed with pickaxes tried to cut away the ice, but just about as soon as they did so, the water simply froze again.

After several months stuck on the ship in this manner, Shackleton had to face the daunting reality that had presented itself. Forced to act or lose everything, Shackleton finally made the fateful decision to abandon ship in late October 1915 when the ship began to take on water through cracks in the hull. Shouting to his crew that "She's going down!" Shackleton directed his men to move as much equipment—including lifeboats and other auxiliary craft—as they could to a temporary encampment on the pack of ice they were trapped upon. After this transfer was made, the crew saw the last of the *Endurance* sink beneath the icy surface on November 21, 1915.

The crew would wait it out for about another month on this ice floe before Shackleton gave the orders to pick up their gear and attempt to make a trek across the frozen waters to nearby Paulet Island, which had previously served as a supply depot. With yet another window of opportunity closing, by December 29, it appeared that the drifting ice they were traversing would not allow them to get anywhere near Paulet Island. The crew would be more or less stuck on the ice floe that had them bound for the next few months with no escape in sight.

Things came to a head on April 9 when the frozen plateau they were encamped upon began to break in half. Ernest Shackleton, knowing that he had to act, didn't hesitate. He immediately ordered everyone into their lifeboats for a last mad dash to the closest island they could reach. It was after five challenging days in the turbulent icy waters that Shackleton and company, manning three separate lifeboats, arrived at the remote locale of Elephant Island. Though a known place, Elephant Island was definitely off the beaten path, and as such, the odds were exceedingly low that anyone would find them on this chilly isle.

Shackleton knew full well that they could starve or freeze to death on this island without anyone ever knowing what had even happened to them. Refusing to relegate his crew to such a fate, he decided to use one of the auxiliary craft in an attempt at one last escape, this time back to South Georgia Island, which was from their vantage point some 720 miles away.

Instead of taking all three boats, Shackleton had a handpicked crew board the largest of the rescue craft—a 20-foot lifeboat called the *James Caird*. Shackleton and his team disembarked from Elephant Island on April 24, 1916. It took over two weeks of painstaking navigation, but on May 9, the crew arrived in the vicinity of South Georgia Island. They were still out of sight of the whaling outposts on the northern shore, but rather than risk another journey by boat, Shackleton determined to take on the arduous task of crossing the island by land. It took a hike of some 36 hours over treacherous terrain, but the station was finally reached on May 20.

From here, Shackleton quickly set into motion the rescue mission to get the rest of his crew still trapped on Elephant Island. With the help of a Chilean tugboat called *Yelcho* and a British whaling craft called *Southern Sky*, the team that had stayed behind on Elephant Island was picked up on August 30, 1916. If anyone had ever snatched victory from the jaws of defeat, Ernest Shackleton could certainly claim to have done so.

Conclusion

Upon Shackleton's return to civilization after his latest polar attempt, he found the world he returned to much changed. The isolated conflict that had broken out when he had left Britain had turned into a worldwide conflagration without any easy end in sight. The First World War would indeed consume almost every aspect of life, and it wasn't long after his return that Shackleton himself—though past the age of the average soldier—would attempt to serve his country in its time of crisis.

He proved to be a great recruiting tool in both Britain and other nations that had joined the Allied war effort. In the lecture tours he frequently gave, Shackleton framed support of the war as not just patriotism but a moral obligation. On one occasion, he went so far as to state, "To take your part in this war is not a matter merely of patriotism, not a matter merely of duty or of expediency; it is a matter of saving a man's soul and of a man's own opinion of himself."

After the war's conclusion in 1918, Shackleton continued to conduct lectures and wrote a book about his time spent on the *Endurance*. Yet rather than just writing about his adventures, Shackleton longed for the real thing. By 1920, he was already speaking of carrying out a new mission. Gaining a new sponsor—an old wealthy friend by the name of John Quiller Rowett—Shackleton began plans for what would become known as the Shackleton-Rowett Expedition, whose stated objectives were to circumnavigate

Antarctica, as well as taking a closer look at some previously unexplored sub-Antarctic islands.

In what would be Shackleton's final expedition, the Shackleton-Rowett crew launched on September 24, 1921. In this last mission, 47-year-old Shackleton was pushing himself to the limits, and his health appears to have suffered as a consequence. Shortly after his team pulled into Rio de Janeiro to prep for their southward launch, it is believed that he may have had a heart attack.

Nevertheless, denying further medical care, Shackleton pressed on, and from Rio, the crew pulled into the old familiar whaling station of South Georgia on January 4, 1922. This was as far as Ernest Shackleton would make it on his last quest, and sadly enough, he would die just one day later. He sustained another more massive heart attack from which he was unable to recover. Shackleton may not have been able to conclude his mission, but even as his body failed him, his spirit soared. With his very last breath, Ernest Shackleton was pushing the limits of exploration, leaving the world in absolute awe in his wake.

Bibliography

Davis, Linda (2009). *Sir Ernest Shackleton* (Great Explorers).

Huntford, Roland (1985). *Shackleton*.

Johnson, Rebecca L. (2003). *Ernest Shackleton: Gripped by the Antarctic*.

Marcovitz, Hal (2001). *Sir Ernest Shackleton and the Struggle Against Antarctica* (Explorers of New Worlds).

Mill, Hugh Robert (1923). *The Life of Sir Ernest Shackleton*.

Shackleton, Ernest (1919). *South*.

Wilson, Edward A. (1975). *Diary of the Discovery Expedition*.

Printed in Great Britain
by Amazon

44068087R00031